# AMERICAN QUILT TREASURES

# AMERICAN QUILT TREASURES

## Historic Quilts from the International Quilt Study Center & Museum

Martingale
Create with Confidence

American Quilt Treasures: Historic Quilts from the
International Quilt Study Center & Museum
© 2017 by Martingale & Company®

Martingale®
19021 120th Ave. NE, Ste. 102
Bothell, WA 98011-9511 USA
ShopMartingale.com

Printed in China
22 21 20 19 18 17          8 7 6 5 4 3 2 1

Library of Congress Cataloging-in-Publication Data is
available upon request.

ISBN: 978-1-60468-891-7

## MISSION STATEMENT

We empower makers who use fabric and yarn
to make life more enjoyable.

## CREDITS

**PUBLISHER AND
CHIEF VISIONARY OFFICER**
Jennifer Erbe Keltner

**CONTENT DIRECTOR**
Karen Costello Soltys

**MANAGING EDITOR**
Tina Cook

**ACQUISITIONS EDITOR**
Karen M. Burns

**COPY EDITOR**
Sheila Chapman Ryan

**PRODUCTION MANAGER**
Regina Girard

**COVER AND
INTERIOR DESIGNER**
Adrienne Smitke

**PHOTOGRAPHER**
Brent Kane

# CONTENTS

**INTRODUCTION**
6

**GALLERY OF QUILTS**
8

**DEDICATION**
143

**ABOUT THE INTERNATIONAL**
**QUILT STUDY CENTER & MUSEUM**
144

# INTRODUCTION

*What defines American quilts? Fabrics? Patterns? Techniques? Workmanship? The people who make them? Those who sleep under them?*

Quilts have become quintessentially American objects, but they have not always covered Americans' beds. Once Americans got started making quilts, they developed a special relationship with them. Americans have produced quilts in a multitude of formats, and for a variety of purposes, from practical to symbolic. Wholecloth, mosaic, medallion, block style, Crazy, utility, prizewinning, political, crib, bed, wall—Americans have created quite a variety.

The business of American quiltmaking in the early twenty-first century is the most recent chapter of a 400-year story of global trade, technological innovations, and entrepreneurial imagination. Cotton is the "thread" that holds the story together. European traders brought home cotton textiles from Asia in the 1600s. The convenience and beauty of these vibrant, colorfast, and wash-fast textiles created a demand that eventually resulted in a revolutionized textile industry that initiated the Industrial Age in Europe and North America.

Entrepreneurs saw opportunity. In the 1840s, a few enterprising women in Baltimore, Maryland, were the source for elaborate appliqué kits using the era's abundant array of printed cotton fabrics. Fifty years later, the Ladies Art Company of St. Louis, Missouri, became the first to offer catalogs of quilt patterns available by mail.

U.S. quilt businesses thrived in the twentieth century. By 1930, large publishing businesses and independent businesses—many owned by women—offered patterns, kits, and completed quilts for sale through newspapers, magazines, and printed catalogs.

Whether sewing alone or in a group, whether designing a unique piece or following a traditional pattern, whether working as a professional or a hobbyist, quiltmaking is a creative act. Traditional quilts often follow a block or grid format. As a result, people sometimes think they are simply a product of imitation and repetition, lacking in true creativity. Anyone who has made a quilt, however, knows creation always involves individual choices. And many quiltmakers over the centuries have only loosely followed patterns, if at all. Each new generation has shaped quiltmaking. As societies, cultures, and individuals have changed, so have quilts. Collectors, scholars, and curators have advanced fresh perspectives on the significance of quiltmaking as an American folk art.

Through quilts, Americans have done a very human thing: they have shared their lives, comfort, and convictions with their families, communities, and strangers. Throughout American history, quiltmakers have used quilts' comforting and unobtrusive qualities to communicate political and social messages. Mid-nineteenth-century Album and Signature quilts, for example, were often made to mark family and community events.

The majority of quilts in the International Quilt Study Center & Museum (IQSCM) collections have unknown makers. Yet we should not consider these quilts simply "anonymous." The families and communities from which they came no doubt celebrated the makers' skill and artistry. And in diverse ways, the quilts reflect their makers' identities.

Whether or not you visit the IQSCM in person or view pieces of our collection only through the pages of this book, we hope you enjoy these specially curated American quilts. Imagine their makers and the creative choices that were made. We know the inspiration they bring continues.

**Spiderweb or Wild Goose Chase Variation**
Possibly made in Ohio, circa 1890, 74" × 75". Maker unknown.

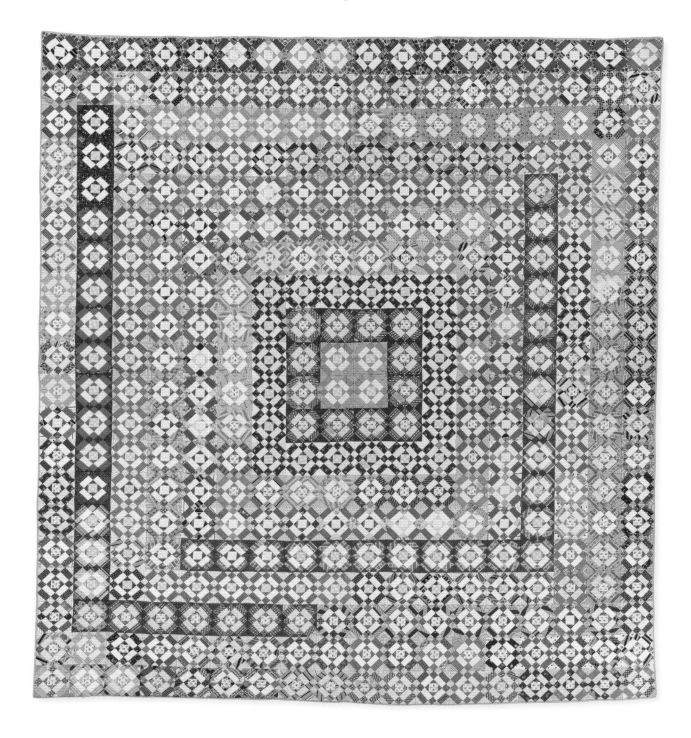

**NINE PATCH VARIATION**
PROBABLY MADE IN NEW ENGLAND, CIRCA 1880, 86" × 94". MAKER UNKNOWN.

**WHIG ROSE**
PROBABLY MADE IN FAYETTEVILLE, TENNESSEE, CIRCA 1900, 83" × 84". DELL PATTERSON.

**TRIP AROUND THE WORLD**
MADE IN KANSAS CITY, KANSAS, CIRCA 1900, 80" × 88". IDA PRICILLA WILLIAMS GIEBNER.

**BALTIMORE ALBUM**
PROBABLY MADE IN BALTIMORE, MARYLAND, CIRCA 1850, 106" × 106". MAKER UNKNOWN.

**IRISH CHAIN VARIATION**
PROBABLY MADE IN NEW ENGLAND, CIRCA 1880, 67" × 78". MAKER UNKNOWN.

**SPIDERWEB**
PROBABLY MADE IN UNION COUNTY, OHIO, DATED MARCH 1936, 70" × 77". MAKER UNKNOWN.

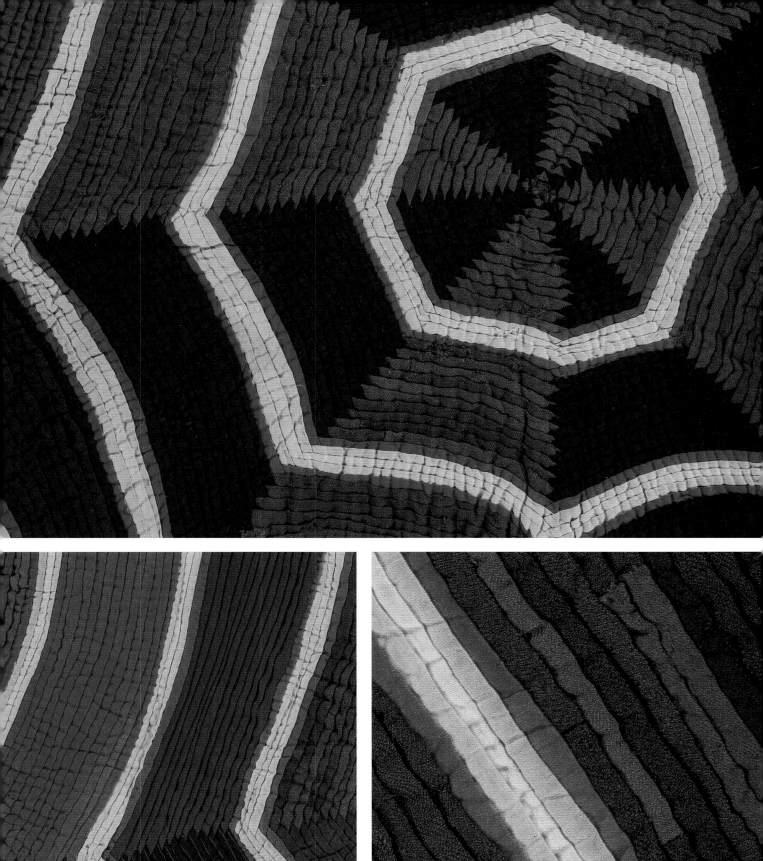

**SAMPLER**
MADE IN LANCASTER COUNTY, PENNSYLVANIA, CIRCA 1880, 88" × 88". SALINDA RUPP.

**SCHERENSCHNITTE**
MADE IN THE UNITED STATES, CIRCA 1860, 81" × 97". INITIALED B.J.

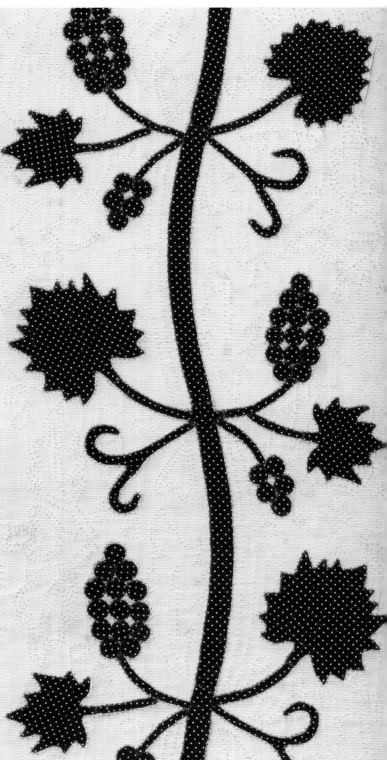

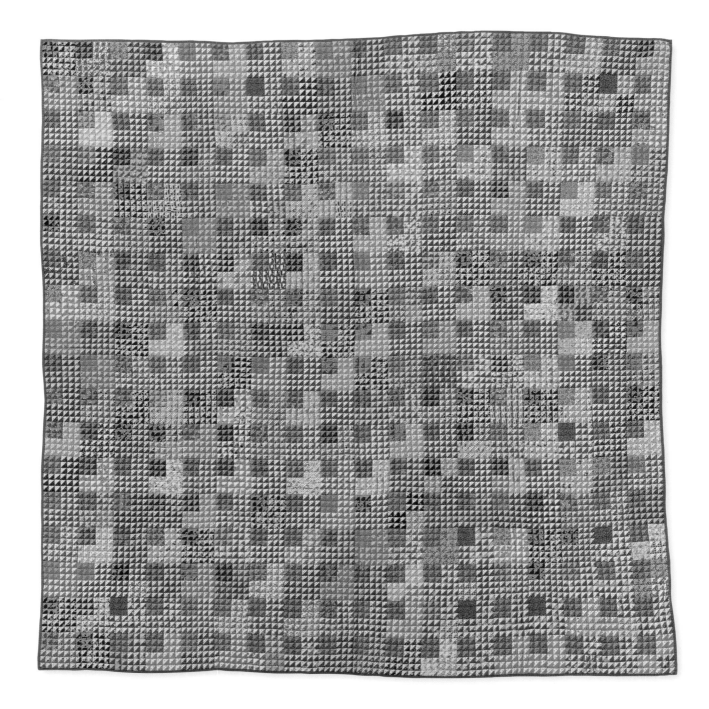

**BIRDS IN THE AIR**
POSSIBLY MADE IN NEW JERSEY, CIRCA 1890, 83" × 86". MARY LINDERBURGER.

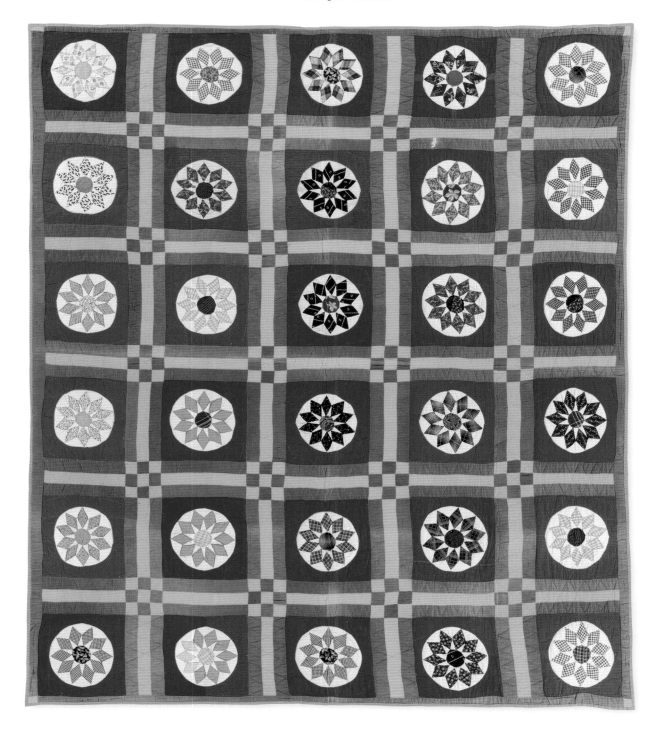

**KANSAS SUNFLOWER "FOUR GENERATION QUILT"**
MADE IN GOTHENBURG, NEBRASKA, DATED 1905–1965, 89" × 89". MULTIPLE MAKERS.

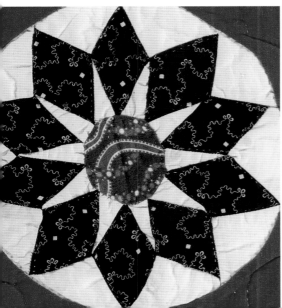

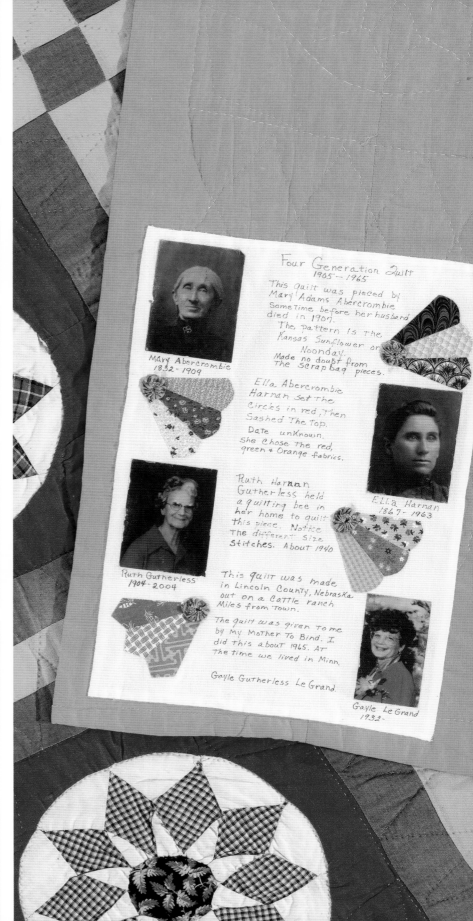

Four Generation Quilt
1905 – 1965

This quilt was pieced by Mary Adams Abercrombie Sometime before her husband died in 1909.
The pattern is the Kansas Sunflower or Noonday.
Made no doubt from The scrapbag pieces.

Mary Abercrombie
1832 – 1909

Ella Abercrombie Harman set the circles in red, Then sashed The Top.
Date unknown.
She chose the red, green & Orange fabrics.

Ella Harman
1867 – 1963

Ruth Harman Gutherless held a quilting bee in her home to quilt This piece. Notice the different size stitches. About 1940

Ruth Gutherless
1904 – 2004

This quilt was made in Lincoln County, Nebraska out on a Cattle ranch Miles from town.

The quilt was given to me by My Mother To Bind. I did this about 1965. At the time we lived in Minn.

Gayle Gutherless Le Grand.

Gayle Le Grand
1932 –

**DIAMOND FIELD**
MADE IN THE UNITED STATES, CIRCA 1895, 77" × 90". L. CORDELIA MALLOW AND HANNAH MALLOW.

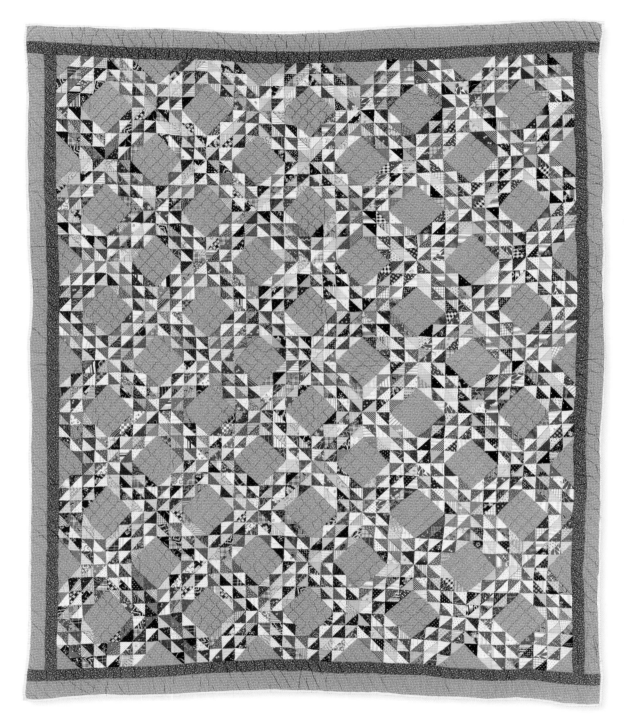

**OCEAN WAVES**
POSSIBLY MADE IN NEBRASKA, CIRCA 1900, 63" × 78". MAKER UNKNOWN.

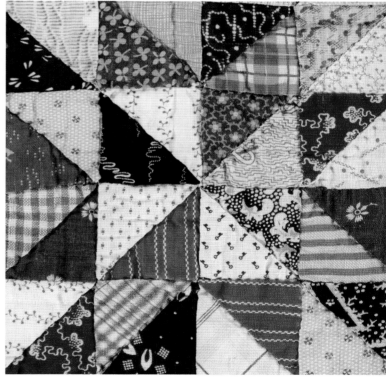

**STATE FLOWERS**
MADE IN NOBLESVILLE, INDIANA, DATED 1932, 79" × 84". EDA R. SHARPE.

**Prairie Point Bull's Eye**
Possibly made in Tennessee, circa 1960, 76" × 87". Maker unknown.

**SNOWFLAKES**
MADE IN THE UNITED STATES, CIRCA 1963, 78" × 92". MAKER UNKNOWN.

**Log Cabin "Crosses"**
Made in Baltimore, Ohio, dated 1976, 93" × 94". Nancy Crow.

**DOUBLE IRISH CHAIN**
MADE IN BENTON, NEW YORK, DATED 1853, 81" × 100". RHODA E. SMITH NUTT.

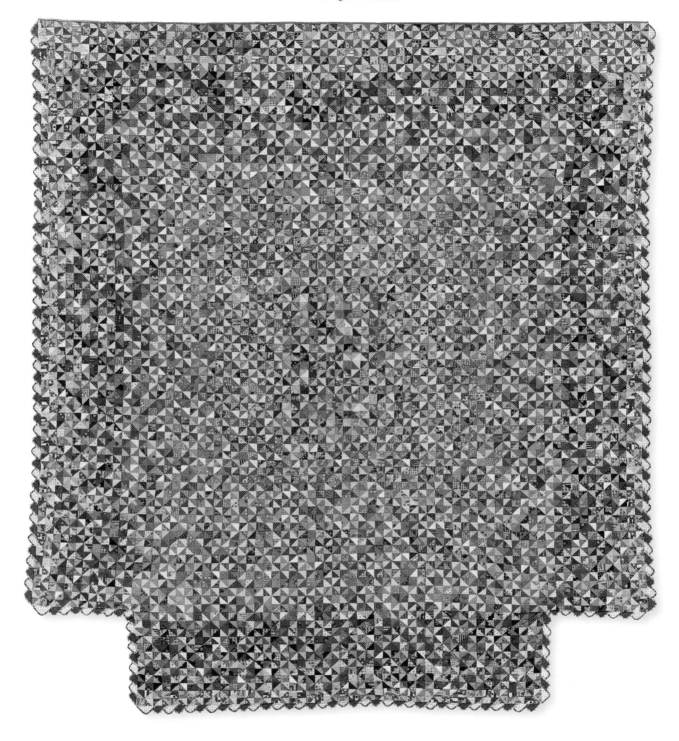

**BROKEN DISHES**
POSSIBLY MADE IN NEW ENGLAND, CIRCA 1870, 77" × 87. MAKER UNKNOWN.

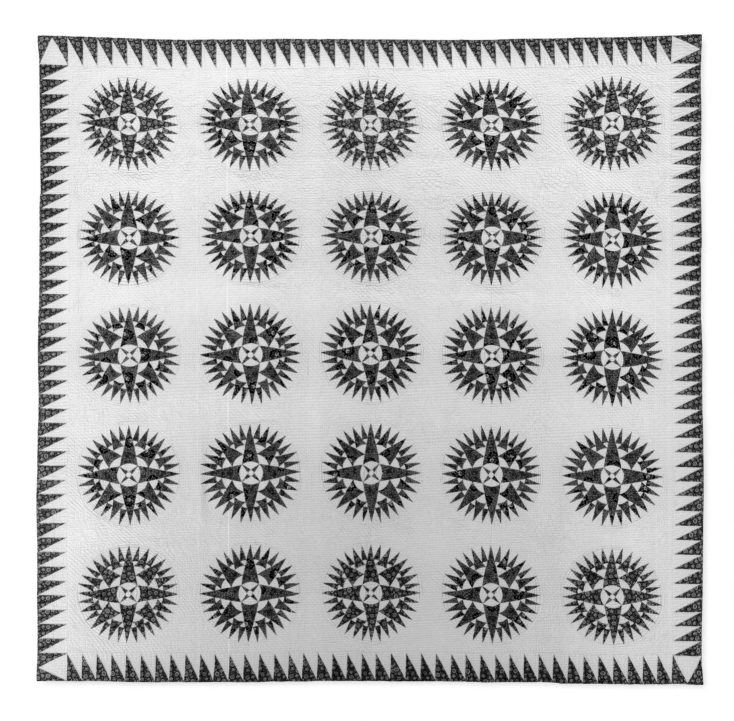

**MARINER'S COMPASS**
POSSIBLY MADE IN SHARON, PENNSYLVANIA, CIRCA 1830, 105" × 107". MAKER UNKNOWN.

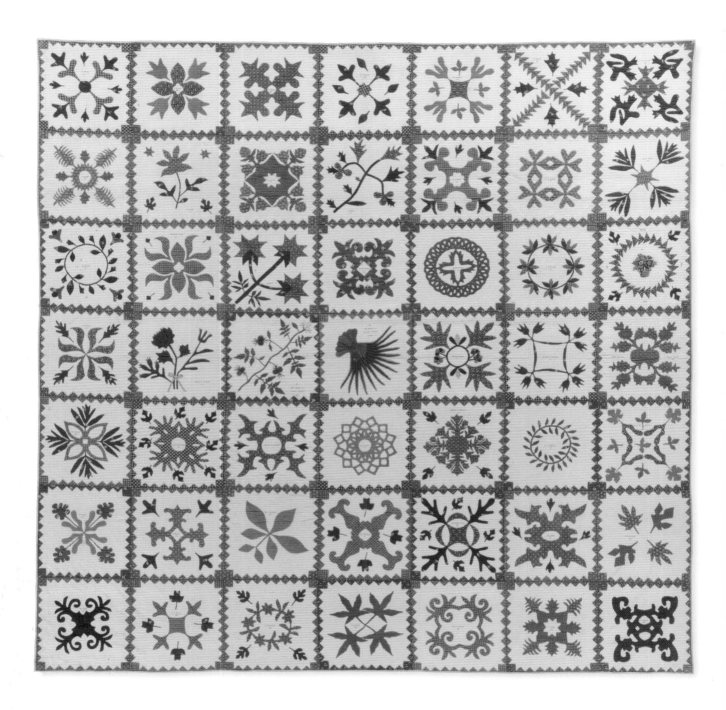

**ALBUM**
MADE IN BALTIMORE, MARYLAND, DATED 1845, 95" × 95". HARGEST FAMILY.

**PINE TREES**
MADE IN THE UNITED STATES, CIRCA 1890, 74" × 76". MAKER UNKNOWN.

**FEATHERED STAR**
MADE IN FRANKLIN COUNTY, OHIO, DATED 1852, 82" × 98". REBECCA ELLEN SLYH.

May the 21 AD 1852
Jesus permit thy gracious name to stand
As an effort of A youthful hand
write thy name upon my heart
And with thy dear children let me share a part.

REBECCA ELLEN SITH.

FRANKLIN COUNTY

OHIO.

**INDIAN HATCHET AND WINDMILL**
POSSIBLY MADE IN OHIO, CIRCA 1910, 70" × 80". MAKER UNKNOWN.

**POPPY**
MADE IN THE UNITED STATES, CIRCA 1930, 78" × 90". MAKER UNKNOWN.

**ONE PATCH**
POSSIBLY MADE IN PENNSYLVANIA, CIRCA 1880, 77" × 85". MAKER UNKNOWN.

**BLAZING STAR**
PROBABLY MADE IN NASHVILLE, ILLINOIS, CIRCA 1890, 82" × 93". MAKER UNKNOWN.

**Log Cabin**
Possibly made in Pennsylvania, circa 1920, 80" × 82". Maker unknown.

**BALTIMORE ALBUM**
MADE IN BALTIMORE, MARYLAND, DATED 1850, 104" × 106". MADE FOR MARY UPDEGRAFF.

**PINEAPPLE**
POSSIBLY MADE IN OHIO, CIRCA 1880, 71" × 71". MAKER UNKNOWN.

**CRAZY QUILT "MY CRAZY DREAM"**
MADE IN BOSTON AND HAVERHILL, MASSACHUSETTS, DATED 1877–1912, 69" × 74".
MARY M. HERNANDRED RICARD.

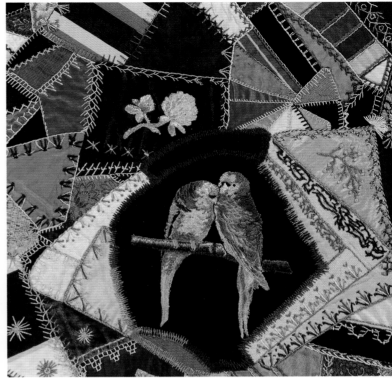

**HAWAIIAN APPLIQUÉ**
PROBABLY MADE IN HAWAII, CIRCA 1940, 81" × 85". MAKER UNKNOWN.

**LOG CABIN VARIATION**
MADE IN EUTAW, GREENE COUNTY, ALABAMA, CIRCA 1987, 91" × 95". AUGUSTA DUNCAN.

**ALBUM**
PROBABLY MADE IN OSSINING, NEW YORK, DATED MAY 1, 1857, 80" × 91". MAKERS UNKNOWN.

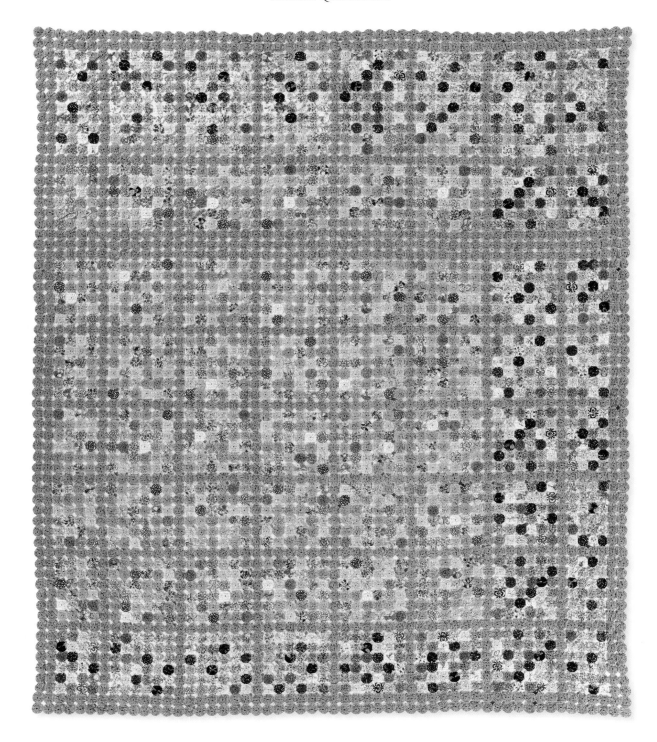

**Yo-Yo**
MADE IN THE UNITED STATES, CIRCA 1950, 92" × 108". MAKER UNKNOWN.

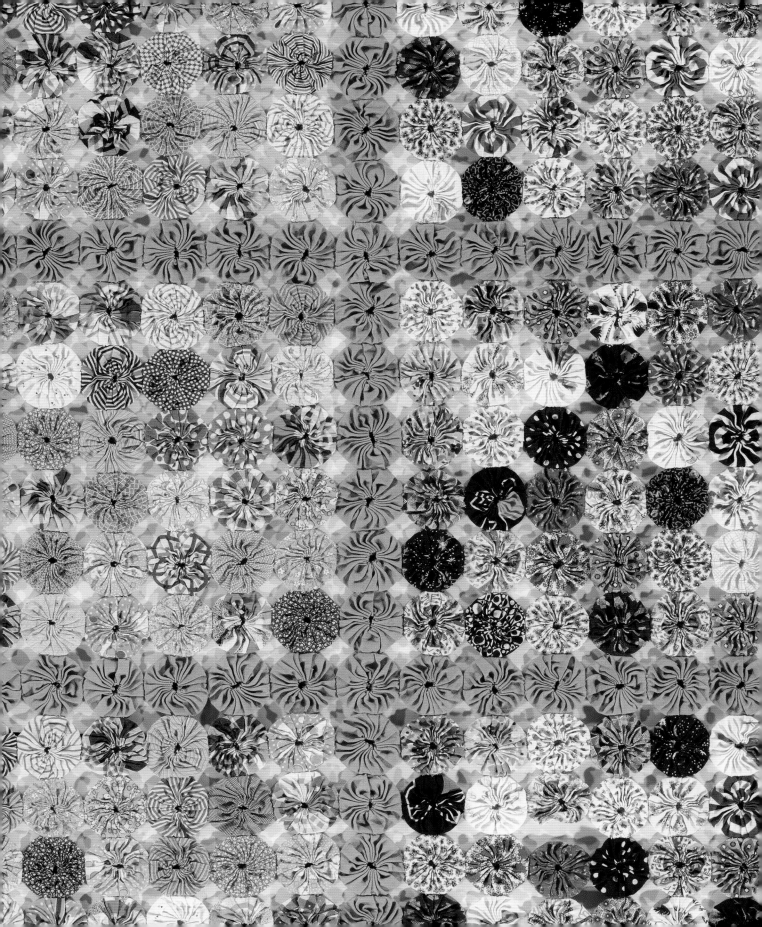

**Star of Bethlehem**
Possibly made in eastern Pennsylvania, circa 1850, 92" × 94". Maker unknown.

**ALBUM "RECONCILIATION QUILT"**
MADE IN BROOKLYN, NEW YORK, DATED 1867, 85" × 97". LUCINDA WARD HONSTAIN.

*Named at some later date, "The Reconciliation Quilt" depicts many family members of the quiltmaker—her husband, brother, daughter, and son-in-law. The quilt derives its name from the block (above) depicting the "reconciliation" between Jefferson Davis and his daughter following his release from prison after the Civil War. The quilt held the record for the most ever spent for a quilt at auction at the time of its purchase in 1991— $264,000.*

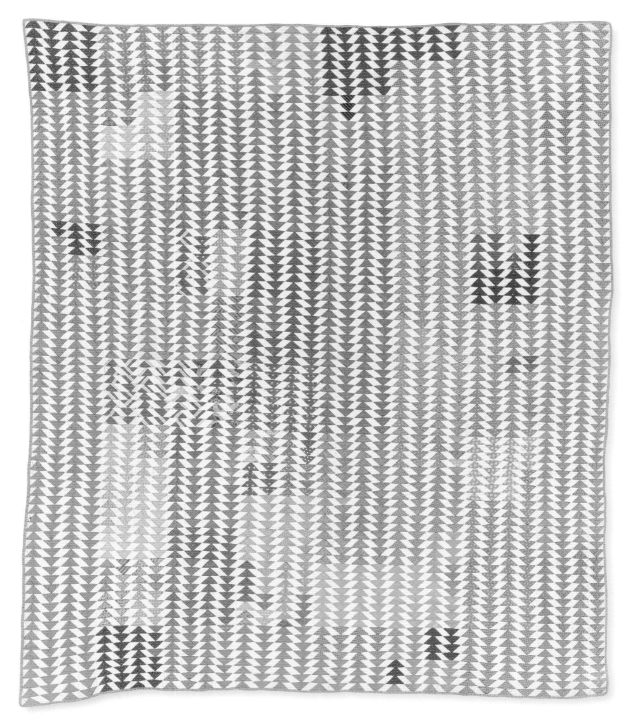

**FLYING GEESE**
MADE IN THE UNITED STATES, CIRCA 1860, 71" × 83". MAKER UNKNOWN.

**APPLIQUÉ**
PROBABLY MADE IN LANCASTER COUNTY, PENNSYLVANIA, CIRCA 1880, 88" × 89". LEHMAN FAMILY.

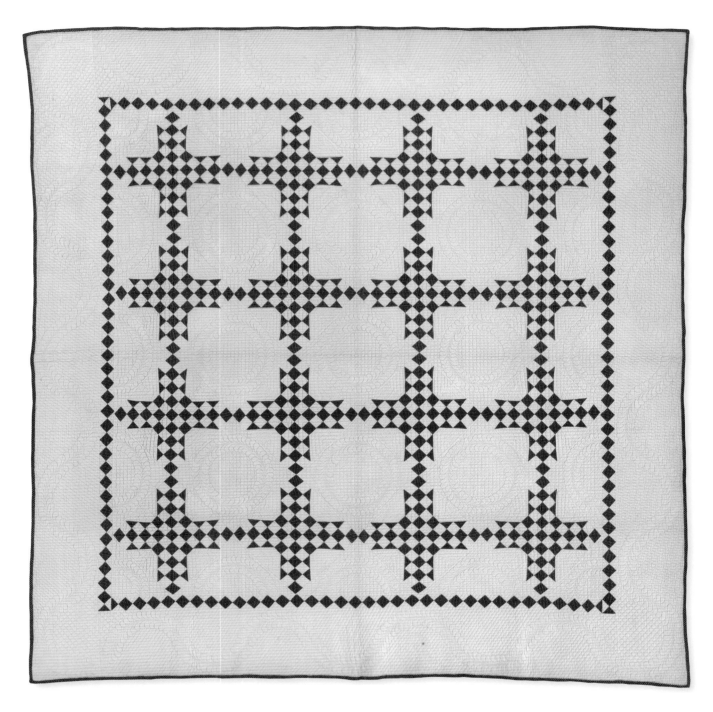

**Reverse Irish Chain**
Possibly made in Cincinnati, Ohio, circa 1870, 77" × 79". Maker unknown.

**SUMAC**
PROBABLY MADE IN PENNSYLVANIA, DATED 1859, 87" × 103". MAKER UNKNOWN.

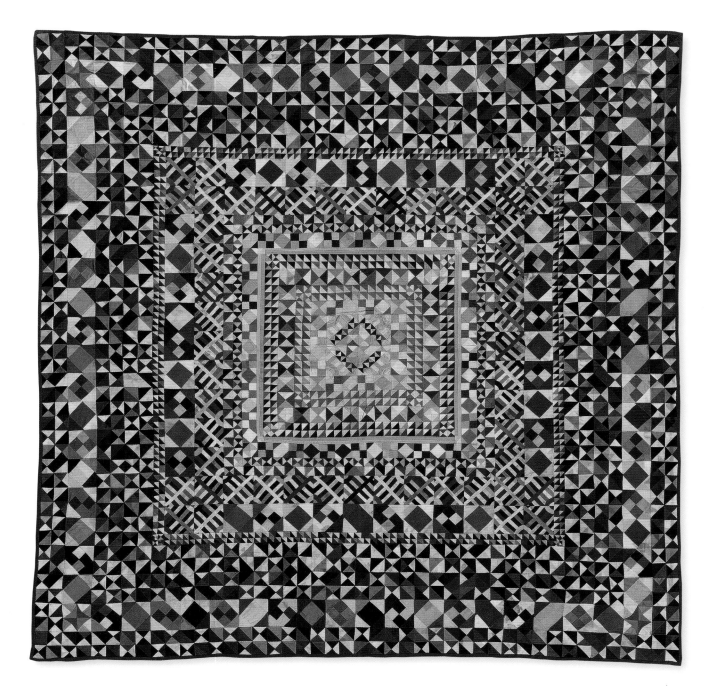

**Patchwork Medallion**
Made in Lincoln, Nebraska, dated 1909–1914, 75" × 77". Bertha Neiden.

**CHINTZ APPLIQUÉ MEDALLION**
PROBABLY MADE IN THE UNITED STATES, CIRCA 1830, 123" × 124". MAKER UNKNOWN.

**POTS OF FLOWERS**

PROBABLY MADE IN PENNSYLVANIA, CIRCA 1849, 87" × 88". LYDIA A. HERMAN.

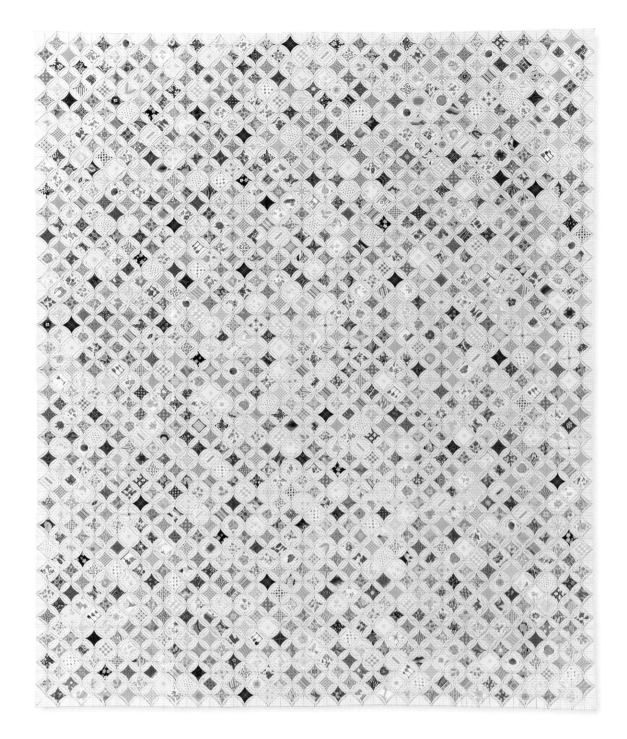

**CATHEDRAL WINDOWS**
MADE IN NEWTOWN, CONNECTICUT, DATED 1974, 71" × 89". VERN F. KNAPP.

**INTARSIA**
PROBABLY MADE IN THE UNITED STATES, CIRCA 1860, 120" × 115". MAKER UNKNOWN.

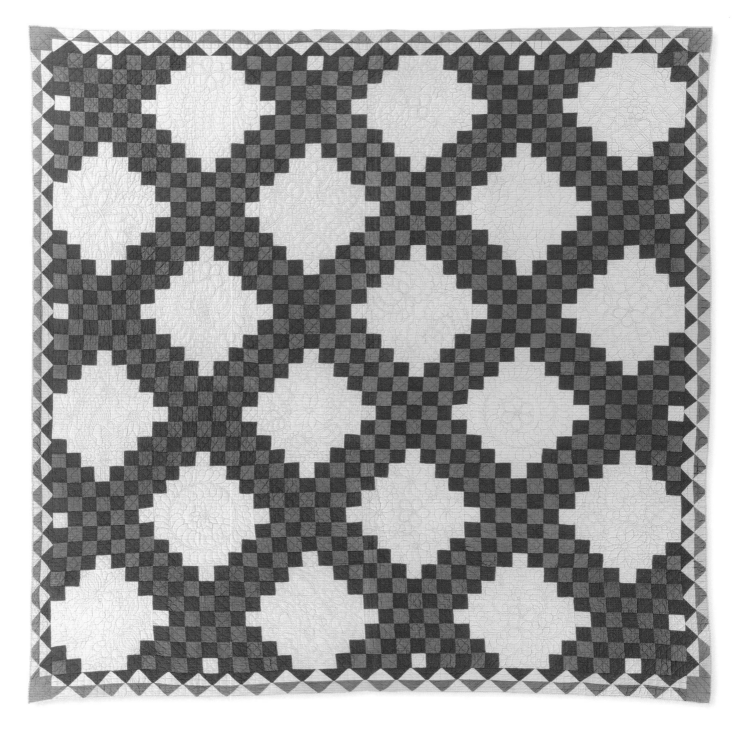

**TRIPLE IRISH CHAIN**
POSSIBLY MADE IN TOWSON, MARYLAND, CIRCA 1870, 82" × 85". MARY ELIZABETH MCCAULEY.

**SUNBURST VARIATION**
POSSIBLY MADE IN PENNSYLVANIA, CIRCA 1820, 95" × 96". MAKER UNKNOWN.

**WREATH OF ROSES**
POSSIBLY MADE IN INDIANA, CIRCA 1930, 59" × 83". MAKER UNKNOWN.

**DOUBLE WEDDING RING**
POSSIBLY MADE IN PICKENS COUNTY, ALABAMA, CIRCA 1970, 68" × 81". MAKER UNKNOWN.

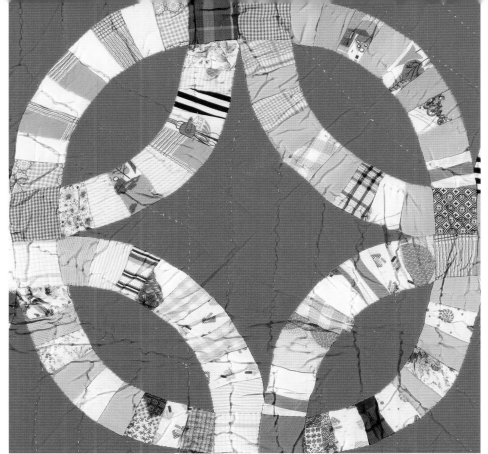

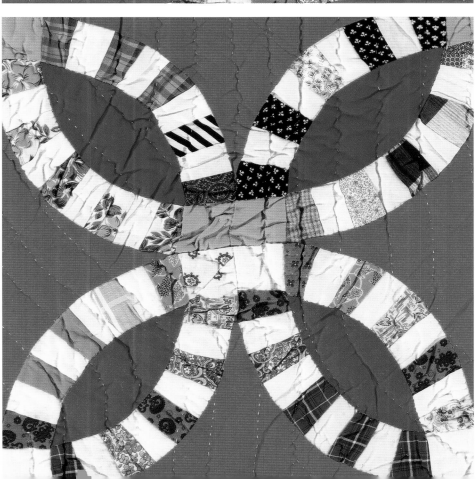

**PATCHWORK ALBUM**
MADE IN PENNSYLVANIA, DATED 1842, 130" × 131". MADE FOR SARAH WISTAR.

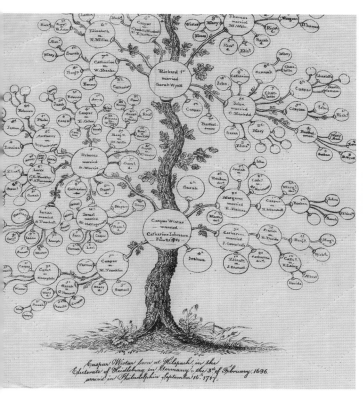

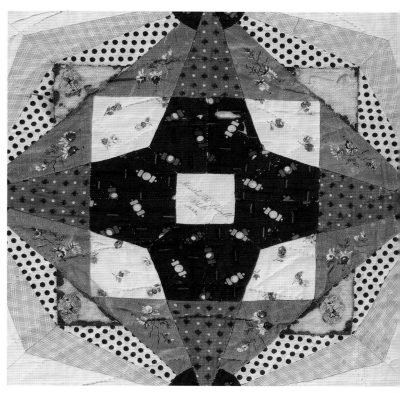

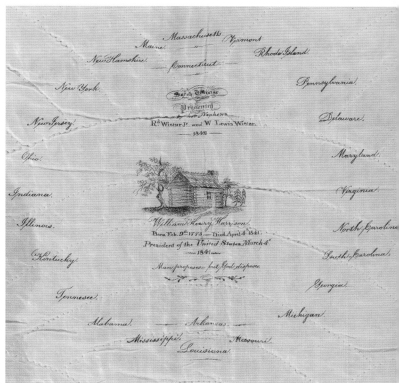

**TRIANGLES**
PROBABLY MADE IN THE UNITED STATES, CIRCA 1870, 72" × 78". MAKER UNKNOWN.

**MEDALLION**
PROBABLY MADE IN THE UNITED STATES, CIRCA 1860, 84" × 96". MAKER UNKNOWN.

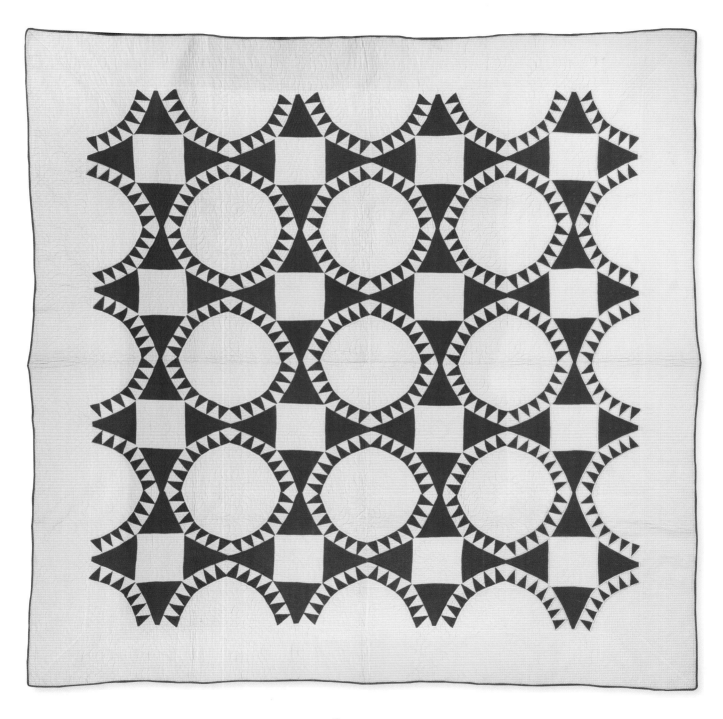

**SUNBURST**
POSSIBLY MADE IN UNION COUNTY, PENNSYLVANIA, CIRCA 1885, 84" × 85". MAKER UNKNOWN.

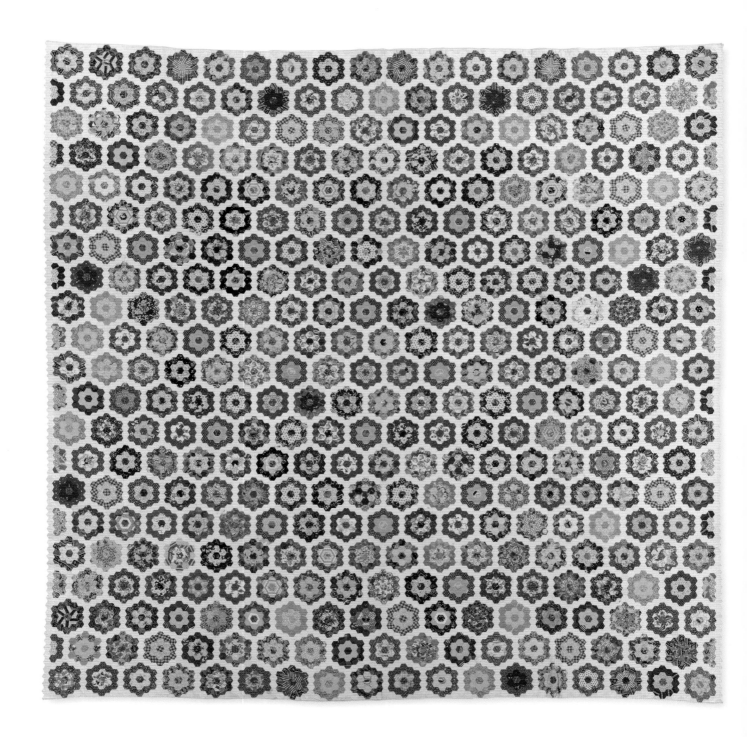

**HEXAGON**
POSSIBLY MADE IN BALTIMORE, MARYLAND, CIRCA 1840, 99" × 99". MAKER UNKNOWN.

**ALBUM**
MADE IN THE UNITED STATES, CIRCA 1920, 87" × 87". MAKER UNKNOWN.

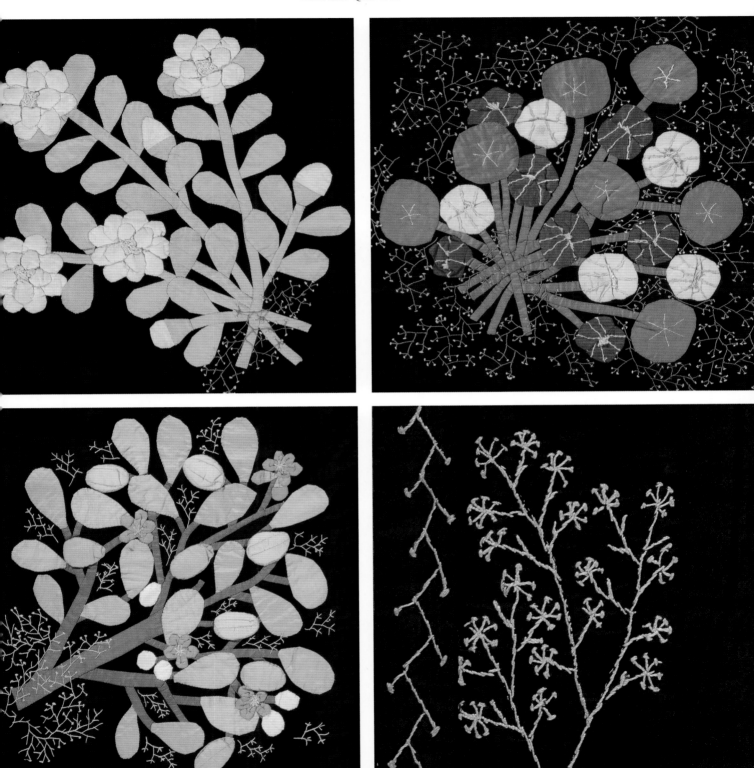

**MARINER'S COMPASS**
MADE IN LINCOLN, NEBRASKA, DATED 1986, 70" × 96". MARY GHORMLEY.

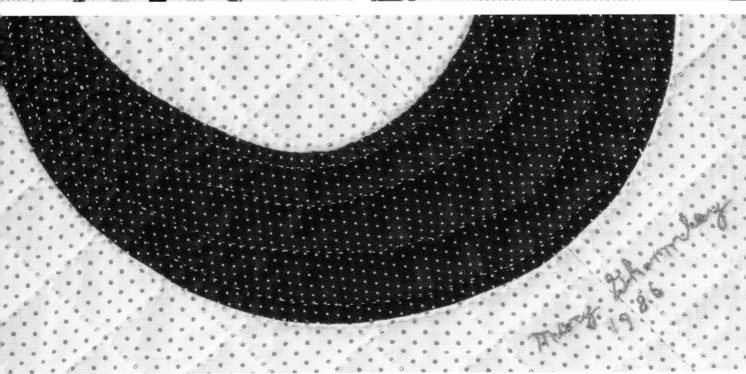

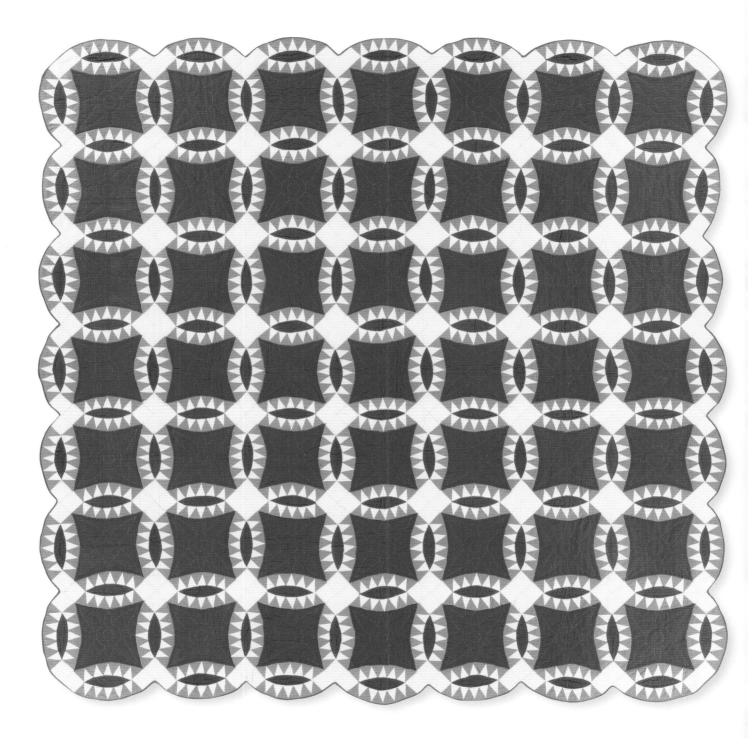

**PICKLE DISH**
POSSIBLY MADE IN OHIO, CIRCA 1940, 83" × 83". MAKER UNKNOWN.

**SWEETHEART "FRIENDSHIP" QUILT**
MADE IN KANSAS CITY, MISSOURI, CIRCA 1940, 80" × 85". MARY ELIZABETH SHELBY.

**PINEAPPLE**
POSSIBLY MADE IN LANCASTER COUNTY, PENNSYLVANIA, CIRCA 1875, 77" × 78". MAKER UNKNOWN.

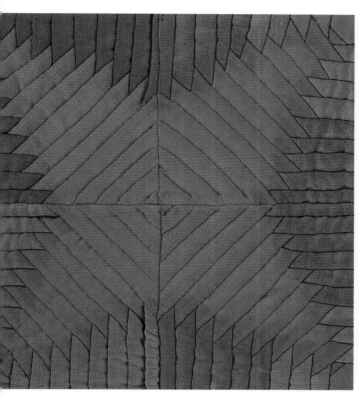 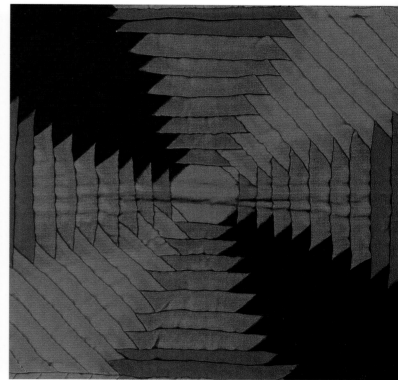

**Coxcomb**
Made in Lawrence County, Pennsylvania, circa 1930, 78" × 80". Cora Arabelle Eckles Dinsmoore.

**HEXAGON MOSAIC**
MADE IN MCPHERSON COUNTY, NEBRASKA, DATED 1940, 98" × 105". GRACE MCCANCE SNYDER.

**SPRINGTIME IN THE ROCKIES**
POSSIBLY MADE IN MARYLAND, CIRCA 1935, 73" × 91". MAKER UNKNOWN.

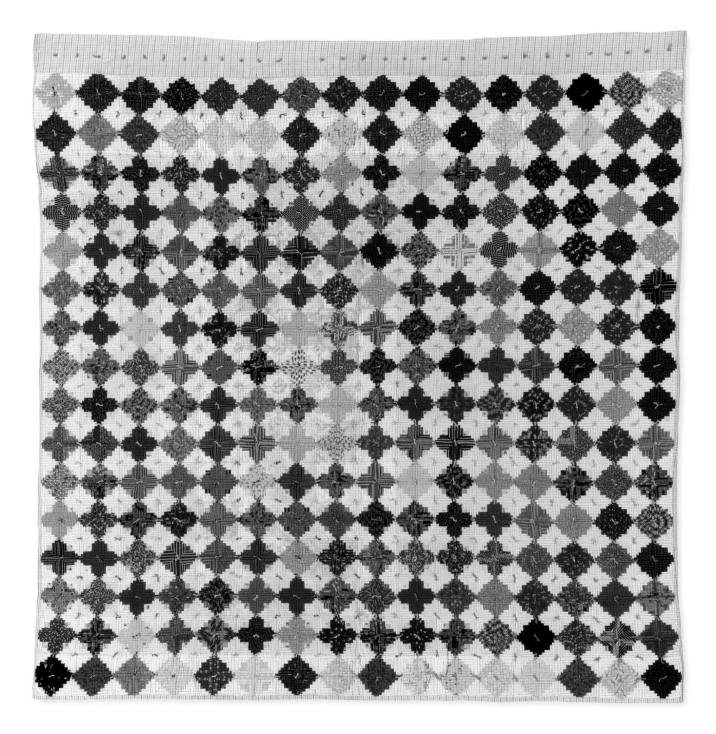

**LOG CABIN**
PROBABLY MADE IN NEW ENGLAND, CIRCA 1900, 71½" × 75". MAKER UNKNOWN.

**FLORAL APPLIQUÉ**
POSSIBLY MADE IN PENNSYLVANIA, CIRCA 1860, 87" × 102". MAKER UNKNOWN.

QUILT HOUSE

DEDICATED TO THE PEOPLE OF NEBRASKA
AND TO QUILTERS AND QUILT LOVERS
EVERYWHERE WHO HAVE MADE THE
DREAM OF AN INTERNATIONAL
QUILT HOUSE A REALITY.

-ARDIS AND ROBERT JAMES

## DEDICATION

The International Quilt Study Center was established in June 1997, when native Nebraskans Ardis and Robert James donated nearly 1,000 quilts from their private collection and an endowment to the University of Nebraska–Lincoln. During the center's early years, the Ardis and Robert James Collection of Antique and Contemporary Quilts was stored in a renovated climate-controlled space in the Home Economics Building on UNL's campus. The IQSC used these quilts, along with other additions to the collection, to create exhibitions that were displayed in galleries on campus and around the world. In 2008, the International Quilt Study Center & Museum moved into a 37,000-square-foot building with three exhibition galleries and state-of-the-art textiles storage. The museum was built with private funding received through the University of Nebraska Foundation, including a lead gift from the James family. More than 130 quilt guilds and quilt organizations in three other countries provided gifts for the building's construction. The IQSCM opened a 13,000-square-foot expansion in June 2015. The new addition doubled the museum's gallery and storage space. The expansion was made possible by a gift from the Robert and Ardis James Foundation as part of the Unversity of Nebraska Foundation's Campaign for Nebraska.

ALBUM "BIG BLUE"
MADE IN CHAPPAQUA, NEW YORK,
DATED 1980, 80" × 92". ARDIS JAMES.

International Quilt Study Center & Museum
University of Nebraska–Lincoln  www.quiltstudy.org

The International Quilt Study Center & Museum's mission is to build a global collection and audience that celebrates the cultural and artistic significance of quilts. The museum has the world's largest publicly held quilt collection, with quilts dating from the early 1700s to the present and representing more than 50 countries. In 2013, the IQSCM received accreditation from the American Alliance of Museums, the highest national recognition a museum can receive.

We envision the 50,000-square-foot IQSCM as a dynamic center of formal and informal learning and discovery for students, teachers, scholars, artists, quilters, and others. Our comprehensive and accessible collection of quilts, related textiles, and documents form a primary text for study, insight, and inspiration.

Located on the University of Nebraska–Lincoln's East Campus (at 1523 N. 33rd St., Lincoln, NE 68583), IQSCM is part of the Department of Textiles, Merchandising & Fashion Design in the College of Education and Human Sciences. The department offers a unique masters degree in Textile History with a quilt studies emphasis, which is the only program of its kind in the world.